It's Your Call

Contents

Haydn Middleton
Character illustrations by Jon Stuart

OXFORD

Taking care of planet Earth

Look around you. How many people can you see? On planet Earth you are very rarely all alone. There are more than six billion people sharing this world. A billion is a thousand million. It looks like this: 1,000,000,000.

The world's **population** is rising faster than ever. By 2050 there could be nine billion of us living on Earth!

Some parts of our world – especially our cities – are already very crowded. But some parts of our world are almost empty. So, surely there must be enough room for everyone? Well, yes, there probably is. That's not our biggest problem.

Our towns and cities are packed with buildings, machines and vehicles. They all use a lot of power. The world's **natural energy** sources are being used up and the waste we produce is making our **environment** more and more **polluted**.

Many scientists believe that pollution is making the Earth warmer. This **global warming** is changing the world's weather. Extreme weather – such as droughts, floods or hurricanes – can have a devastating effect on some countries.

Severe weather like these floods in Bangladesh, might make some parts of our planet **uninhabitable**.

It's Your Call

We need to take care of this precious planet of ours. Let's face it, we haven't got anywhere else to live. Each one of us can do something to help.

This book makes some suggestions. You may not like them. Or you may think they could help keep the world in good shape for future generations.

Time for a clear-out

It's the school holidays. You're bored. So bored, that you offer to clear out the garage. It's FULL of junk!

You find:

- A box full of bottles and jars
- A pile of magazines
- A bag of your old clothes
- Two mobile phones.

You know that glass containers and paper can be **recycled**. So you put the bottles, jars and magazines in a special box. The **council** collects this box every week and takes the materials to be recycled.

In the UK, we recycle about half of our glass waste.

Recycling tips

Glass containers:

- Wash the container out before recycling
- Remove metal or plastic lids
- NEVER put broken glass out for recycling.

Recycled glass is used to make:

- New jars and bottles
- Sand.

You look through the bag of clothes. There is nothing wrong with them – they're just too small for you now. You put them to one side to take to a charity shop. Someone else might want them. It saves throwing them away.

Finally, you look at the mobile phones. No one uses them any more. No one else will want them. You put them in a bag to go out with the rubbish. What harm can a couple of mobile phones do anyway?

Mobile Menace

This image was created on a computer. It shows 426 000 mobile phones. That is the number of mobiles that people in the USA throw out every day. You might only have two phones in your rubbish bag – but remember there are six billion of us!

Cellphones by American artist Chris Jordan, 2007.

Household rubbish that cannot be recycled, or rubbish that people don't bother to recycle, gets crushed and buried in big pits called *landfill sites*. Some of the buried rubbish – like food and paper – rots away. Some rubbish – like plastics and metals – will never rot. It stays buried in the ground forever.

The good news is ... mobile phones can be recycled. There are many charities that will take old or unwanted handsets. If the handsets work, they send them to people in poorer countries who can't afford mobile phones. If the handsets don't work, the different parts can be recycled.

Mobile phones don't rot. So just think how many mobile phones are piling up in landfill sites like this all over the world.

It's Your Call

SO ... the question is: landfill or recycle?

Watch out for water

You've been out in the park playing ball games with your friends. It was great fun, but the ground was really muddy and you're filthy from head to toe. Now you're home you need to get yourself and your kit cleaned up.

You decide you will need:

- The hosepipe – to rinse off your trainers
- The washing machine – to wash your clothes
- A nice big bath – to get yourself clean.

Water, water everywhere!

Without fresh water to drink people, plants and animals can't survive. Today we use about ten times more water than we did a hundred years ago.

Why is that? Well, it's partly because there are more of us. But it's also because **technology** has made getting and using water much easier. Today, millions of pipes carry water directly to our homes. We turn on a tap and there it is. You even have a choice – hot or cold!

When water is this easy to get, it makes the supply seem endless.

However, in some countries water is very **scarce**. There are no pipes or taps. Some adults and children have to walk many kilometres every day to collect fresh water for their families. Water is very precious and is only used for essential drinking, cooking and cleaning.

These girls are carrying water over 3 kilometres uphill, to their homes in Haiti.

Save it – or else!

Almost three quarters of our planet is made up of water – so there should be plenty to go round, right? Wrong! Most of this water is in the world's oceans and ocean water is very salty. People and most plants and animals cannot drink salty water.

We rely on rainfall and the fresh water in rivers and streams to supply the water we need to survive. As our planet gets warmer, the rivers and streams dry up. It won't be long before there is not enough fresh water to go round.

Water saving tips

Here are some things every one of us can do every day to save water.

- Use a bucket and a sponge – not a hosepipe – to clean things outdoors like your bike or your dirty shoes.
- Don't fill a bath, take a shower. This will use less water.
- Turn off the tap when you're brushing your teeth.
- Fit a water-saving device inside your toilet.
- Only use the washing machine when it's full.
- Collect rainwater and use this to water the garden.

Make sure you always turn a tap off properly. A leak of just one drop per second could waste nearly ten thousand litres of water in a year!

This device is called a Hippo. It helps to cut down the amount of water used when the toilet is flushed.

It's Your Call

SO ... the question is: hosepipe and hot bath or a sponge and a shower?

The trouble with travel

You live in a village. To get to the shops and to your school you have to travel two miles to the nearest town. It takes about 5 minutes in the car. But is this really the best way to travel? How long does it take to travel two miles?

Are we poisoning our air?

As the Earth's population increases, so does the number of cars, trucks and lorries on our roads. There are nearly 34 million vehicles on the UK's roads alone. Almost all of these vehicles are powered by petrol or diesel. Petrol and diesel are **fuels** made from oil. When these fuels burn inside a car engine, they produce waste gases such as carbon dioxide. These waste gases – called fumes – pass out through the exhaust pipe and into the air.

Clean, fresh air is as important to us as clean, fresh water. Exhaust fumes from cars pollute the air around us and can make us sick. Pollution from traffic fumes is also one of the major causes of global warming.

Our travel choices

For every one of us, our travel choice is about deciding what is most important – getting somewhere quickly, getting somewhere safely, or protecting the environment for future generations. Here are some arguments for and against different ways of getting around.

Travel choice	Arguments for	Arguments against
Walking	• Doesn't cause pollution • Keeps you fit and healthy • It's free!	• Not very fast so you can't travel far on foot • Not easy if you need to carry lots of shopping or have small children • Not easy if you find walking difficult • Can be dangerous near busy roads or in the countryside where there are no footpaths or street lights.
Cycling	• Doesn't cause pollution • Keeps you fit and healthy • Much quicker than walking • Lots of cycle paths in towns and cities make cycling safer • It's cheap.	• Not easy if you need to carry lots of shopping or have small children • Not easy if you find cycling difficult • Can be dangerous on busy or unlit roads, or if you don't wear the proper protective clothing • It can be difficult to find somewhere safe to leave your bike.
By car	• You can travel where you want, when you want • You can carry things easily – including other people • It's usually the quickest way to get around.	• Fumes from cars pollute the air • On congested roads, travel can be slow in a car • Cars are expensive to buy and run • Not everyone can drive a car.

Travel choice	Arguments for	Arguments against
By bus	• One bus can carry as many people as eight cars • Anyone can travel on a bus – modern buses are accessible to people with pushchairs and disabled people • In most places, buses run all day, nearly every day • Special bus lanes in towns and cities allow buses to go past all the cars • Bus travel is cheaper than having a car.	• Fumes from buses pollute our air – buses with only a few passengers are just as bad for our environment as cars • Buses only run at certain times – so you have to travel when the bus does • Buses can get busy – if the bus is full, you have to wait for the next one • In some areas, particularly in the countryside, buses don't run very often • Some buses take the long way round – they pick up lots of people, but they take much longer to get there.

This is a 'hybrid' car – it has an engine and a battery. When the car is powered using the battery, it doesn't release any fumes into the air.

It's Your Call

SO ... the question is: walk, bike, bus or car?

Dinner damage

You are in a large supermarket. There is a lot of food to choose from, especially fruits and vegetables. It is autumn, so there are lots of apples and berries and potatoes. There are also fruits and vegetables from all over the world. Fruit is good for you, right? You decide you'd like some strawberries. You pick up a box and look at the label. It says: Produce of New Zealand.

The price of choice

A banana farmer is packing fairtrade bananas ready to send abroad.

Supermarkets offer a wide range of foods from all over the world. Most of the fruits and vegetables that grow in the UK are *seasonal*. This means that they grow only at certain times of the year. At other times of the year we have to **import** foods such as strawberries and tomatoes. Some of our favourite fruits like oranges, mangoes and bananas only grow in hot countries. They have to be imported all year round. *Ninety-five* per cent of the fruit and half of the vegetables in the UK are imported.

Some of the fruit travels thousands of kilometres by truck, plane, boat and train to get to our supermarkets. These vehicles all burn fuel which pollutes our atmosphere (see pages 13–15).

Air pollution is a huge problem, but it's not the only reason why food that travels long distances is bad for the environment.

In some underdeveloped countries, large areas of land are **cultivated** in order to produce food for **export**.

This is a map of South America. The Amazon spans nine countries and covers some 5.5 million kilometres.

The Amazon rainforest is the largest rainforest in the world. It is a dense tropical forest in South America which is home to an amazing variety of animal and plant life.

Large areas of the rainforest are being cut down for agricultural production. Crops – like soya – are grown in its place and exported across the world. This takes up land that could be used to grow food for local people. It is also having a devastating effect on the rainforest. Trees are not replanted and this destroys **habitats** for plants and animals.

Should we ban imported food?	
Yes	**No**
Imported food is not necessary for a healthy diet. We can produce what we need locally. A ban would encourage people to eat seasonal foods.	Importing food gives us choice. We can have a range of fresh fruit and vegetables all year round. This gives us a more varied diet.
Growing food abroad destroys large areas of land that could be used to feed poor people in that country. It also destroys the habitat for many plants and animals.	A ban on imported food would have a devastating effect on poor people in the developing world who rely on exports to survive. Many people would lose their jobs.
Imported food causes a lot of damage to the environment because of the pollution released during transportation.	Less energy is used in growing crops in the developing world. The better climate means that a greater variety of fruit and vegetables can be grown.

It has been estimated that if deforestation is not stopped, then by 2050 40% of the Amazon rainforest will have been destroyed.

It's Your Call

SO … the question is:
buy local or imported food?

Electric shock

One evening, you are in your room watching TV. You want to use the Internet later to check your emails, so you've left the computer on standby. Your mobile phone is plugged in and recharging. There is a light on above you and a lamp on by the computer.

Village lights up ... at last!

In June 2003, the last place on the UK mainland without electricity finally got their power switched on. After a long campaign, the residents of the small village Cwm Brefi, a valley in the Cambrian mountains in west Wales, finally got connected to the **national grid**. Before then, they had to use **generators** to power their homes.

We now use twice as much power in our homes than we did 30 years ago. Why is that? It's a bit like the water supplies (see pages 8–11). Today, most of us take electricity for granted. You flick a switch and there it is. It gives us light and heat and powers many of the machines and gadgets we have come to depend on.

Technology is changing the way we live. New machines and gadgets are being invented every day to help us do things, make things and have fun! All of these gadgets have one thing in common – they need electricity to make them work.

The source of power

All electric power has to come from somewhere. Before it gets to your house, it has to be created in power stations. Most power stations currently run by burning **fossil fuels**, like coal, gas and oil. These are all *natural resources* which means that they occur in nature.

There's a problem though. Natural resources are *non renewable* which means that once we have used them, that's it, there are no more. All over the world, we're using so much coal, gas and oil that we're in danger of running out of our natural resources.

This is a coal fired power station in China. Nearly a quarter of the world's electric power is used for lighting. You'd have to burn 600 000 tons of coal a day to make that much power.

Running out of natural resources is not the only problem, though. Burning fossil fuels creates a lot of air pollution. The pollution goes into the **atmosphere** and can cause breathing problems in people. It can also turn into **acid rain** which is harmful to freshwater lakes and forests.

Fossil fuels also release carbon dioxide when they are burned which is a major **greenhouse gas**. This may be contributing to global warming (see pp 28–30).

A diagram to show the effects of burning fossil fuels.

We need to find *renewable* sources of energy – this means things that can be used over and over again without running out. We also need to find environmentally friendly alternatives to using fossil fuels – ones that don't damage the environment.

Powerful alternatives

Solar

You've just heard something exciting on TV. We don't need to rely on fossil fuels – we can use the sun instead! How? By putting solar panels on our roofs. The sun will warm them and create power that can help to heat and light our homes.

This picture shows some solar panels in Utah, USA.

As with most forms of power, there are pros and cons to using solar energy. Fitting your home with solar panels can be quite expensive and many people cannot afford this. Others are not convinced that solar panels will generate all the power we need. So what else can be done?

Wind

Wind is another source of renewable energy. *Wind farms* are becoming more common. A wind farm uses lots of big wind *turbines*. These turbines normally have 3 blades. The blades face the wind and the wind forces them to go round. This turns a shaft inside the turbine which is connected to a generator. This generator produces the electricity.

Turbines stand between 25 and 80 metres in height.

A field of rapeseed.

Biofuels

Biofuels are made from living things or from the waste they produce. This includes things like wood, straw and animal waste. In recent years, more crops have been grown to make biofuel – such as corn, sugarcane and rapeseed. These crops can be made into ethanol and diesel which is used mostly in transport.

Nuclear

Nuclear power is a complicated chemical process that produces electricity. A lot of electricity can be produced and some people believe it is the only way that we will be able to produce enough of the energy we need. It doesn't release as many greenhouse gases or other acidic air pollutants, but many people still argue that it is not safe because of the radioactive waste the power stations produce.

A nuclear power station.

Some of the pros and cons

Energy Source	Pros	Cons
Solar panels	• Solar panels help save money on electricity bills in the long-term • Solar panels don't give off any pollution • Solar energy can still be used on overcast or dull days • You don't need to be linked to the national grid. Homes in remote areas can still get electricity.	• The cost of putting solar panels on your roof is very expensive • The weather can affect the efficiency of solar cells • Solar energy is only able to generate electricity during the day • Solar panels take up a lot of space.
Wind farms	• Wind turbines don't produce chemical or radioactive emissions • If the turbines need to be taken down, there is no damage to the environment • The land around the turbines is still safe for agricultural purposes, like for grazing sheep.	• Many people don't like having wind turbines near where they live. They also think they ruin the landscape and are noisy • Wind farms take up much more space than normal power stations in order to produce the same amount of energy • Wind farms can be costly to run.
Biofuel	• Biofuels are largely renewable. This means that they will not run out • Biofuels can cut greenhouse gas emissions • They are easy to adapt to our current technology.	• Growing more crops for fuel will mean more land is needed. This will destroy more habitats for animals and plants • If more food crops are used for fuel, it may push up food prices • Engines cannot fully cope with these new fuels at the moment.
Nuclear power	• Nuclear power produces much more energy than fossil fuels • Nuclear power stations produce fewer greenhouse gas emissions than fossil-fuelled power stations.	• Waste from the power plants is extremely toxic. There is no safe way to store it or dispose of it • Transporting nuclear fuel can be risky.

What you can do to help?

Powerful advice

Here are just some of the things you can do in your own home to help save electricity:

- Turn off all lights that you are not using
- Use low energy light bulbs
- Always shut down your computer when you are not using it
- Don't leave your mobile on all night to charge – only leave it on for a few hours
- Don't leave the TV on standby – turn it off when you're not using it
- Only boil the kettle once if making a hot drink
- Make sure you don't leave the fridge or freezer door open for long periods of time
- Shut windows and doors to keep heat in.

It's Your Call

SO ... the question is:
what will you do to save energy?

Global Warming

Most scientists now agree that our world is getting warmer. They call this *global warming*. If this continues, it could be disastrous for planet Earth.

We are all contributing to global warming. When we burn fossil fuels to get power, gases escape into the sky – they wrap around our world like a blanket.

The sun's rays get through to warm the earth. These rays then get trapped by the blanket of gases and cannot escape back to space. This means that our weather keeps getting warmer. Some places could soon be too hot and dry to live in. Other places could be too wet.

Remember what you learned about water? Almost three quarters of our planet is made of water. Some of it has frozen to form ice. If the planet warms up, the ice will melt back into water. All that extra water will need to find somewhere to go.

This means that sea levels will rise and water will spill on to the land. Coastal towns and cities could flood – and some of them might disappear forever.

Ice is already melting at the North Pole. If the ice disappears so will animals like this polar bear.

These glaciers could be lost forever if the world warms up.

IT'S YOUR CALL ...

You could look at the world's problems and feel too small to have an effect. But if everyone helps to make a small difference, the effect could be enormous!

Remember you can help:

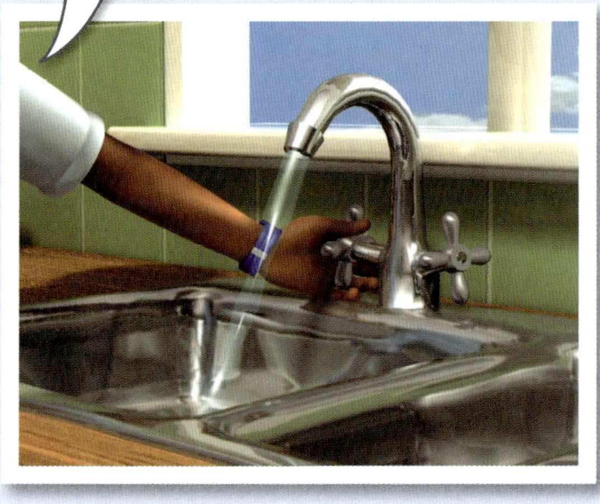

Glossary

acid rain	rain that is made acidic which can damage the environment
atmosphere	the air around the earth
council	a group of people set up to run a city, county or district
cultivate	to prepare and use land for growing crops
environment	the world we live in, especially the plants, animals, and things around us
export	to send goods to another country
fossil fuels	a natural fuel such as coal or gas that has been made from fossils of dead plants or animals that have been in the ground for millions of years
fuel	material that is burned to produce heat or power
generator	a machine that can produce electricity
global warming	the gradual warming-up of the world's temperature
greenhouse gas	a gas that traps the sun's rays in the atmosphere
habitat	where an animal or plant lives
import	to bring goods into a country
national grid	the network of power lines that links power stations together
natural energy	power that comes from nature, like from the sun
pollute	to make air, water and other things dirty
population	the number of people who live in a place
scarce	not enough, not often found, rare
recycle	to use paper, glass, or other things again instead of throwing them away
technology	studying machines and how things work
uninhabitable	unsuitable for living in

Index